A GUIDE TO PUBLISHING
IN SCHOLARLY
COMMUNICATION JOURNALS

Third Edition

by Mark L. Knapp and John A. Daly
University of Texas at Austin

International Communication Association

Lawrence Erlbaum Associates
Taylor & Francis Group

New York   London

Loyola University Library

Published by

Lawrence Erlbaum Associates, Inc., Publishers
10 Industrial Avenue
Mahwah, New Jersey 07430

Cover design by Kathryn Houghtaling Lacey

ISBN 0-8058-4952-1 (pbk. alk. paper)

Books published by Lawrence Erlbaum Associates are printed on acid-
free paper, and their bindings are chosen for strength and durability.

Printed in the United States of America
10 9 8 7 6 5 4 3 2

TABLE OF CONTENTS

THE REVISION AND RESUBMISSION PROCESS 25

APPENDIXES 30

INTRODUCTION

Getting your ideas and research published in a scholarly journal is simply a matter of having good ideas and doing sound research, right? Wrong. Whereas rigorous thinking and methodological precision increase your chances for publication, you must also understand and follow certain rules associated with the publication process. In other words, success in publishing is a result not only of *what* one produces, but *how, when, where,* and *to whom* it is presented.

Those who can tell us the most about journal publishing are the editors, whose success as authors and/or reviewers secured their appointments as editors. With their unique perspective, no other group is better prepared to advise on how to effectively play the publishing game.

In organizing and writing the first edition of this guide, we distilled the collected experiences, opinions, pet peeves, and advice of the 10 scholars and journal editors listed below:

> Robert Avery, *Critical Studies in Mass Communication,* 1984–1986
> Charles R. Berger, *Human Communication Research,* 1983–1986
> Steven Chaffee, *Communication Research,* 1984–1986
> John A. Daly, *Communication Education,* 1985–1987; *Written Communication,* 1983–1990
> B. Aubrey Fisher, *Western Speech Communication Journal,* 1982–1984
> Gustav Friedrich, *Communication Education,* 1979–1984
> George Gerbner, *Journal of Communication,* 1973–1986
> Mark L. Knapp, *Human Communication Research,* 1980–1983
> Thomas McCain, *Journal of Broadcasting,* 1980–1984
> Gerald R. Miller, *Human Communication Research,* 1974–1977; *Communication Monographs,* 1984–1986

Much of the information presented in this guide stems from questions directed at these editors during panel discussions at meetings of professional communication associations. The most welcome responses on these panels were those that spoke directly to demystifying various procedures and apparent biases associated with the publication process. We have tried to adopt this principle for this revised edition as well.

In order to complete and update this edition, we sought advice and counsel from the following editors:

Frank Boster, *Communication Monographs*
Donald Rubin, *Communication Education*
Joann Keyton, *Journal of Applied Communication Research*
Bonnie Dow & Celeste Condit, *Critical Studies in Media Communication*
William Benoit, *Journal of Communication*
James Bradac & Howard Giles, *Journal of Language and Social Psychology*
Jean Folkerts, *Journalism & Mass Communication Quarterly*
Mark Fine, *Journal of Personal and Social Relations*
Tom Lindolof, *Journal of Broadcasting and Electronic Media*
Scott Jacobs, *Communication Theory*
Pam Shoemaker, *Communication Research*
Els de Bens, *European Journal of Communication*
David Henry, *Western States Journal of Communication*
John O. Greene, *Human Communication Research*
Karlyn Kohrs Campbell, *Quarterly Journal of Speech*

The guide begins with an overview of the publication process, followed by discussion of each step of the manuscript submission, review, and revision processes. In addition to reality-based answers to questions often posed to editors, the guide provides other resource material in the appendixes. This guide is specifically designed for those who wish to publish in scholarly journals. The publication process associated with popular, trade, or quasi-academic, profit-motivated magazines has a different set of rules, regulations, and writing requirements.

There are also several manuals about the process of writing a scholarly article. Among these are Luey's *Handbook for Academic Authors* (Cambridge University Press), the *Publication Manual of the American Psychological Association,* Alexander & Potter's *How to Publish Your Communication Research: An Insider's Guide* (Sage), and Huff's *Writing for Scholarly Publication* (Sage). Our focus is less on the process of developing a scholarly article and more on the issues and procedures associated with the publication process.

The guide aims to (1) examine rules and expectations encountered during the publishing process that are often assumed to be known but are not; (2) lead to greater consistency in publication practices; and (3) contribute to increasing the quality of journal submissions as well as the quality of editor and reviewer interaction.

Mark L. Knapp
John A. Daly

THE PUBLICATION PROCESS IN BRIEF

There are two primary motives for scholarly publishing: (1) sharing research findings and (2) advancing a career. Sharing research findings addresses the responsibility of scholars to advance knowledge. Presenting ideas publicly and incorporating, critiquing, and extending the ideas of others provide a forum for developing and refining ideas and an environment in which knowledge of each phenomenon under study progresses through combined effort. Sometimes understanding is slowed as peers provide checks and balances; sometimes knowledge is advanced quickly because many minds are at work on a single problem. Very often, the process of writing for publication forces the author to think about issues and concerns that might not have been considered otherwise.

The second motivation for publishing is more personal. In today's academic world, publishing is the primary route to promotion, tenure, and salary increases. More and more, the committees who make such decisions examine the quality, reputation, and circulation of the journals in which your work is published.

Assuming, then, that you are going to submit your work for publication, the following is an overview of how the process unfolds:

Step 1: Submission
You send your manuscript to the editor listed in the most recent issue of the journal in which you are seeking publication, following published specifications for that journal. The editor will generally notify you within two weeks that the manuscript has been received.

Step 2: Review
Within a couple of weeks, the editor will determine whether or not to send the manuscript out for review. Once a manuscript is sent for review to two or three subject matter experts, the review process takes from two to four months (this varies). With the counsel of his or her reviewers, the editor will make one of three publication decisions: (1) to accept (sometimes contingent on additional revisions), (2) to reject, or (3) to ask for revision and resubmission.

Step 3: Revision and Resubmission
If revised and resubmitted, the manuscript will be reviewed again—often by the same reviewers who examined the original manuscript. Procedures for notifying the author and expected time lags for reviewing the revision are sometimes shorter, but often are the same as for the original submission.

THE SUBMISSION PROCESS
Determining What to Submit
Editors will tell you: "Send me only your best work," but it is up to you to determine what that is. The pressures to publish are often so strong that you might be tempted to submit material before it has received the kind of thought and attention to detail it needs. Editors and reviewers, though, will recognize a spotty literature review or superficial discussion section, and the editor may ask you to provide greater depth to the manuscript or reject it outright. One editor told us that the most common comment from reviewers of manuscripts he rejected was "so what?" Manuscripts that are technically acceptable but do not significantly further our understanding of some aspect   of communication will usually be rejected.

Journals generally publish their submission guidelines, either in the journal itself or on its website, and you would be wise to examine these carefully before deciding whether or not to submit. Some manuscripts, hard as it may be to admit it, are best left in the office file. Submitting a manuscript "just to see if it flies" is a waste of time and effort for author, editor, and reviewer. Submission guidelines often address not only what the editor is looking for in the way of content and style, but also detail how a manuscript is to be submitted.

Conference Papers
Many scholars believe that manuscripts ready for conference presentation are also ready for publication. Some may be, but many are not. Even conference papers that receive awards may be rejected because journals have different needs and standards. One reason is that conference papers are often selected on a comparative basis whereas manuscripts for publication are normally judged on an absolute basis. Highly rated conference papers are often those that were "best" in terms of papers submitted. That standard of excellence may or may not hold up when the manuscript is evaluated for inclusion in the literature of the field.

Timing Your Submission
As it does with many things, timing can play a role in whether or not your article is accepted for publication. Normally, the highest volume of manuscripts is received immediately following submission deadlines for conference papers and during the weeks following professional confer-

ences. Although there are authors who assume manuscripts accepted for conferences are ready for publication, there are other authors who wait to incorporate feedback from the conference into their manuscripts before submitting. Manuscripts submitted during these periods, as well as during holiday or summer breaks, may take slightly longer to process and, with the quantity of manuscripts available during this time, the editor may be less likely to make a close call in favor of a "borderline" manuscript.

Editors also receive a rush of manuscripts (even some previously rejected) at the start of their editorial tenure. Because a new editor will be working to establish high standards, this ploy is not often successful.

Determining Where to Send the Manuscript

The most important principle in determining where to send a manuscript is to match the nature of your manuscript to the nature of the journal. Four factors need to be considered:

1. Level of Scholarly Excellence and Contribution to Knowledge. If your article is of high quality (that is, you think it is some of your best work or some of the best work done in the area, AND some of your colleagues agree), you should send it to a journal with high visibility (international or national circulation) and a reputation for publishing important, quality manuscripts. If you perceive your manuscript to make a more moderate contribution, you may wish to send it to a regional journal, a journal published by a state professional association, or one that has a moderate to low circulation among a specialized group of scholars. Journal quality changes over time, and perceptions of specialized journals are sometimes more favorable than for better known journals. The important thing is to make sure those who evaluate your professional work perceive that your best work landed in quality journals.

2. Subject Matter. Consider subject matter in determining where to send your manuscript. Some journals will specialize in the topic you are addressing; others will publish in that area as well as others. New editors often state in their first issue or on the journal's website what types of manuscripts they are seeking. Although some journals profess to publish in a broad range of areas, they may tend to emphasize some over others. This can work to your advantage (the editor may be looking for articles in an area not frequently represented) or disadvantage (the editor may prefer articles in other areas). Articles that are too different from the typical subject matter of the journal are usually rejected by the editor without review. The best way to determine the range of acceptable topics is to examine the most recent volumes of the journal you are considering. Remember that a paucity of articles on a particular subject may be due to lack of submissions rather than editorial preference. If in doubt, submit to the journal that you prefer.

3. Journal Needs. Journals have special needs. Sometimes these needs are related to the range of publication interests (e.g., book reviews, professional news, colloquies) and sometimes to content. Content needs might concern such things as special themes for future issues forecast in previous issues or professional newsletters; the absence of articles in a particular area for a long period of time; or follow-up on an article that appeared in an earlier issue. Editors also are concerned with the overall conception of an article and how the author's approach fits into the level and scope of research published. The interests of the readership, as well as overall editorial policy, are also factors in shaping a specific issue of a journal.

4. The Image of the Journal Editor. When journal editors are questioned about the content they publish, they frequently resort to saying, "I can only publish what I receive and I do not get many submissions dealing with _____." Authors have preconceptions of editors as well as the journals they publish, and if an editor has become associated with a certain type of research or a particular subject area, he or she is likely to attract submissions of this nature. An editor's first issues create an image of him or her and may affect the type of submissions the journal receives afterward. If an editor disproportionately publishes the research of his or her students, friends, and colleagues or publishes an inordinate number of articles dealing with his or her own research specialty, the range of articles submitted to this journal will likely diminish. In short, both editors and authors—and the conceptions they have about each other—can determine journal content. Even though one emphasis may prevail, this does not necessarily mean other topics or methodologies are not welcome.

Journals often change what they publish as they change editors. For example, not every journal publishes book reviews. Some are more interested in essays, and some in systematic and controlled research projects. Others include news of professional activities, and still others have special sections devoted to such things as instructional practices. To determine what a journal currently publishes, examine issues from the preceding two years. Listed below are several communication associations in the U.S. and elsewhere that publish journals. Refer to their websites for current editorial policies and submission procedures:

International Communication Association
http://www.icahdq.org
Human Communication Research
Journal of Communication
Communication Theory
Journal of Computer-Mediated Communication

National Communication Association
http://www.natcom.org/pubs
Quarterly Journal of Speech
Communication Monographs
Communication Education
Journal of Applied Communication Research
Critical Studies in Media Communication
Text & Performance Quarterly
Review of Communication
Communication and Critical/Cultural Studies

Western States Communication Association
http://www.westcom.org
Western Journal of Communication
Communication Reports

Central States Communication Association
http://www.csca-net.org
Communication Studies

Southern States Communication Association
http://www.ssca.net
Southern Communication Journal

Eastern Communication Association
http://www.ecasite.org
Communication Quarterly
Communication Research Reports

Association for Education in Journalism and Mass Communication
http://www.aejmc.org
Journalism Quarterly
Journalism Educator
Journalism Monographs

American Communication Association
http://www.americancomm.org
American Communication Journal

Broadcast Education Association
http://www.beanet.org
Journal of Broadcasting and Electronic Media
Broadcast Monographs
Feedback

International Institute of Communication
http://www.iicom.org
Intermedia

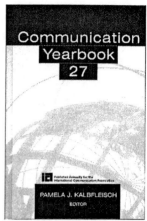

World Communication Association
http://ilc2.doshisha.ac.jp/users/kkitao/organi/wca/journal
Communication Research Reports
World Communication

These are a few of a wide range of journals to which communication scholars may submit their work. An Internet search will reveal many others in communication and other social sciences throughout the world that may be appropriate publication outlets for various types of communication theory and research. *Communication Abstracts* (Sage) publishes brief summaries of articles and books about human communication collected from a variety of sources. Descriptions of many of these journals may be found in C. LaGuardia, W. Katz, & L. S. Katz (Eds.), *Magazines for Libraries* (11th ed.), New Providence, NJ: Bowker, 2002. Tables of contents of more than 1,300 scholarly journals can be found in the weekly publication, *Current Contents: Social and Behavioral Sciences* (Philadelphia: Institute for Scientific Information).

Cover Letters
Generally, cover letters should do no more than state the title of the manuscript and confirm that you would like the enclosed manuscript considered for publication in a particular journal. Occasionally, you may need to explain some aspect of the manuscript, but brevity is the goal. You may want to include the history of your manuscript and assure the editor that it has not been published elsewhere and is not currently under consideration at any other journal. It is unnecessary to write an extensive summary or justification for your article.

Address your cover letter to the correct editor, journal, and address. Making mistakes on these small points reflects on your credibility as a careful scholar and researcher.

Include information that allows the editor to stay in touch with you: your full address, telephone and FAX numbers, and email address if you have one. Include numbers where you can be reached if you are going to be gone for extended periods. Unless the editorial guidelines for a particular journal instruct otherwise, and some do, it is a good idea to put the contact information on the title page of your manuscript as well. Update your information if anything changes.

Some journals have special sections such as research notes or instructional practices. When you submit a piece that you think fits a particular section, you should mention that in your cover letter.

Editors seek impartiality in their decisions and often go to great lengths to avoid the appearance of impropriety. Thus, you should avoid any attempt to use friendship with an editor as leverage for a favorable publication decision. To do so is professionally unethical.

Editors also encounter implicit (and sometimes explicit) pleas from authors based on the author's professional needs. Avoid any statement that even suggests that acceptance of a particular manuscript will get you hired, promoted, or tenured, or otherwise enhance your career. Comments like this are clearly inconsistent with the attempt to evaluate a manuscript on the basis of scholarly merit. See Appendix A for an example of an appropriate submission letter.

Presubmission Reviews

Are presubmission reviews by colleagues necessary? No, but having your manuscript examined by knowledgeable colleagues who will provide useful, candid feedback can help ensure more favorable reviews and even increase the speed with which a favorable publication decision is made. Editors strongly encourage presubmission reviews, and many authors recognize the potential value of seeking them, but surprisingly few actually do.

Presubmission reviewers who merely pat you on the back and say, "Great work!" do little to improve the quality of the manuscript. Be aware that colleagues who are offering informal presubmission reviews may be more encouraging than they would be as anonymous journal reviewers of the same manuscript because of the demands of collegiality. Thus, an author may obtain helpful guidance from presubmission reviews, but such reviews do not guarantee publication.

Whom should you use as presubmission reviewers? Often colleagues in your own department or school can fill this role, although close friends may not provide the kind of objectivity you seek. Authors also may circulate their manuscripts to scholars at other institutions who are acknowledged experts in the topic area the manuscript addresses. Some are hesitant to do this, but it may be the only way for some authors to get presubmission reviews. The presubmission review is an extra step in the usual process, but it can be a worthwhile vehicle for gaining useful feedback that enhances your manuscript's chance of publication.

Simultaneous Submissions

Virtually all scholars consider this practice to be ethically unacceptable, and many journals expressly forbid it. Editors should be able to assume that manuscripts submitted to their journal are not concurrently being considered by any other journal. If you submit a manuscript to more than one journal simultaneously, you should inform each editor that the manuscript is being sent to other journals. Don't be surprised if editors respond by telling you they do not want to go through a long editorial process and ask reviewers to spend many hours evaluating your manuscript if they are competing with other journals. In addition, the stylistic requirements for journals often differ sufficiently so that multiple submissions would pose considerable work for the author. In brief, it is best to avoid this practice.

Preparing the Manuscript

Some scholars will argue that matters of style are trivial compared to the substance of a manuscript. Ideally, this position seems reasonable, but practically, a poor stylistic presentation gives both reviewer and editor an immediate impression that the author has not given the manuscript the time and attention it deserves—which makes them wonder whether they should spend time evaluating the manuscript.

Writing Style. Sloppy writing and presentation are often associated with sloppy thinking, and this is not the impression an author wants to give an editor. One editor-consultant noted:

> As communication scholars, we know that messages have the potential to create an impression of the source in the receiver. Because we use blind review (except when guesses are possible), the impression the reviewer has of the author is created by the manuscript itself. Do you want to be thought of as sloppy and careless, or meticulous? Of course substance is more important than style, but style does matter.

14

Writing style is an important factor in determining a manuscript's worth. Sometimes authors assume that academic writing is inherently dull and as long as there are no technical errors, the writing should be acceptable. There is less tolerance for this position by journal editors today than ever before. Manuscripts can be both intellectually precise and interesting to read—but achieving that takes more effort by authors. Writing that is clear and interesting gives a manuscript a better chance of acceptance—provided that all other standards for acceptance have been met.

Targeting the Right Audience. Identifying the target audience to which you are writing is also important. If an author writes primarily for himself/herself or a small group of like-minded colleagues, the magnitude of the contribution must be greater for the article to be worthy of publication. If the manuscript appeals to a larger audience, editors may see value in less noteworthy treatises.

Theses, student term papers, conference papers, and manuscripts for scholarly journals are all written for different audiences. When a dissertation, term paper, or conference paper is prepared for journal submission, it should be drafted to a particular journal's style and to its readers. In short, it needs to be rewritten for a different audience.

If a manuscript is rejected by one journal and you plan to send it to another, rework the manuscript to fit the style of the new journal. Always check the latest issue (or the website) of the journal to which you are submitting to be sure of current submission requirements. As one of the editor-consultants for this edition put it:

> It is the responsibility of the author(s) to make a case for why a submission should be published, rather than the editor's responsibility to make a case for why it should not. And a part of that case is exercising care and attention to all matters of content and expression.

The Basics. The careful author attends to such basic writing elements as punctuation, grammar, spelling, and organization. Many authors do not proofread manuscripts prior to submission—thinking such minor errors will not detract sufficiently to affect a publication decision. Authors seem particularly prone to such errors with electronic submissions. To be successful as an author, you not only should carefully proof your own manuscripts prior to submission, but also ask another person to read it for errors because it is often difficult to spot errors in your own work. In the case of a borderline manuscript, careful proofing might make the difference between acceptance and rejection.

The Introduction. Authors sometimes underestimate the importance of the introduction. One of our consulting editors made this observation about the importance of the introduction to scholarly manuscripts:

> The introduction is the most important element in the manuscript . . . because it sets the parameters of the study and it lays the foundation for the "so what"? If an author does not draw the boundaries well, reviewers will be confused or will provide suggestions to improve a study that the author has not undertaken. The review process then becomes a frustrating argument where authors and reviewers talk past each other when they fail to connect on the study's purpose. Also, authors who fail to engage in the task of providing a strong justification for their study early on in the manuscript often do not realize themselves that their study is trivial. . . . If more authors paid more attention to the task of writing a good introduction, editors would not receive so many poorly framed manuscripts and the review process would be more constructive and positive for both authors and reviewers.

Overwriting. Overwriting can also be a stumbling block. One of our editor-consultants observed:

> I find too many overwritten manuscripts. One source of the problem, as I see it, is a humanities orientation some authors have. But it is also caused by the inability of an author to make an argument clearly and concisely—presenting premises, evidence, and then drawing plausible conclusions. Another source of this problem is padding references—providing a source for every statement, no matter how generally acceptable it may be. When authors don't test their hypotheses directly they end up having to provide more justification and hedging in the discussion section than is normally warranted.

Getting the References Right. Carelessness in the matter of references and citations inevitably affects reader perceptions of quality. Some common problems include (1) misspelling names; (2) citing authors in the text who do not appear in the reference list at the end of the article (or vice versa); (3) using a citation and reference style other than the one designated by the journal in which publication is sought; (4) failing to double space; and (5) giving an incomplete citation.

Some authors try to impress reviewers by overciting—for example, listing five citations for an idea where one or two key citations would be more appropriate. Instead of increasing the perception of scholarship, overcitation makes the reviewer feel that the author is not discriminating in his or her work (or worse, has not read the sources closely enough to select the most relevant).

Meeting Specific Submission Requirements. To find current submission guidelines, consult the website or the most recent issue of the journal to which you are submitting and follow the guidelines outlined there. Your checklist should include these factors:

- Using the right-sized paper
- Double-spacing the manuscript
- Using the right-sized type
- Leaving appropriate margins
- Sending the requested number of copies in the form specified
- Sending clear, crisp, readable copies
- Using the specified style for references
- Double-checking references for completeness
- Including relevant tables and figures in the submission package

Meeting Length Requirements. If you are asked to reduce the length of your manuscript to meet page requirements, remember that you are being asked to cut out words (content), not simply to reduce spacing, type size, or margins. Using these tricks to make your manuscript appear shorter will usually result in having your manuscript returned to you with another request for you to reduce the content of the article.

> *Editor's Tip: Checking a journal's most recent issue or its website for submission requirements—and then observing them—show respect for the journal and the editor and are definitely in the author's best interest.*

Preparing the Abstract

Abstracts should be understandable to an unsophisticated reader—that is, one who has not just finished reading the article itself. A good abstract will incorporate terms critical to the study so electronic searches will properly catalogue it. Use of jargon, however, should not interfere with understandability. Consider that journal readers process sections of an article in sequence, often title, abstract, introduction, conclusion, method, results, and discussion. Many readers do not complete the sequence, so the title, abstract, introduction, and conclusion may need more attention than would otherwise be given to them.

Sending the Manuscript

Unless you are less concerned than most authors about when and whether your manuscript is received, use first class or overnight mail to ensure timely delivery. Also keep in mind that even first class mail initiated on one university campus and sent to another one may experience delays due to the efficiency of the campus postal systems. Make sure to use sufficient postage and carefully package your manuscript so it will not be damaged in transit. There is no hard and fast preference for stapling or paper clipping manuscripts, but remember that jostling in the mail may cause manuscripts to arrive unattached. If you have camera-ready tables or figures, you may not want to staple these to the rest of the manuscript.

Some journals are moving to an electronic submission process. Check the website of your intended journal to see if electronic submission is required and how that journal wants you to proceed. When sending submissions electronically, be certain not to send documents with a computer virus. That is not a good way to impress an editor.

Follow-up Inquiries

Although not universally practiced, many editors send you a form letter, postcard, or email indicating that your manuscript has been received and is being processed. This notification should also indicate an identifying number assigned to your manuscript. If you want to be sure you'll know the date of receipt, enclose a self-addressed, stamped postcard for the editor to return. If you have not heard from an editor within two or three weeks after you think he/she received your manuscript, you may write a polite letter of inquiry or email mentioning the title of the manuscript and the date it was sent.

Summary of Author/Editor Expectations in the Submission Process

Author

Expects the editor to notify him or her promptly that the manuscript has been received and that the editorial process has begun.

Expects interaction with the editor to be professional in nature.

Expects his/her manuscript to be treated fairly.

Editor

Expects authors to tailor manuscripts to fit stated needs and requirements of the journal.

Expects that this manuscript is not being currently considered by other journals.

Expects the manuscript to be original work.

THE REVIEW PROCESS

Manuscript Evaluation

Normally, an editor will seek written evaluations from two reviewers with expertise in the appropriate content area. If it is an area the editor feels very confident about, he or she may solicit only one other reviewer's opinion to supplement his or her own. If the opinions of the two reviewers are very different (one says reject and one says publish), the editor may solicit a third scholar's opinion unless he/she feels confident in casting the tie-breaking vote. Sometimes the editor has more confidence in one reviewer and gives him/her more credence.

Reviewers are normally asked to complete a form with their evaluation and recommendation (see Appendix B for an example) and to provide written comments supporting their decision. The editor specifies a deadline for completion of the review.

Critics frequently comment on such things as:
- the importance of the manuscript to the subject area and the field in general;
- the thoroughness/relevance of the background material (related literature) reviewed and analyzed;
- the methodological and statistical (when appropriate) sophistication of the project;
- appropriateness of measurement and analytical procedures;
- the extent to which conclusions are properly qualified; and
- writing style (i.e., clarity, interest, and organization).

When editors get a lot of publishable material, the standards associated with each of these six areas get increasingly difficult for authors to meet; on the other hand, when journal pages need to be filled, less stringent standards may be applied.

Reviewers are expected to write critiques that are constructive—ones that they would not mind receiving themselves. However, the amount of time and sensitivity given to a manuscript varies considerably. The reviewer who scribbles something like "This is worthless!" on the evaluation sheet might as well not participate in the process at all, and the editor may avoid using this reviewer in the future. Similarly, the editor will often complement helpful comments by a reviewer with observations of his/her own. The editor has a great deal of control over the nature of the reviews he or she receives by the instructions he/she gives to reviewers. Appendix C provides an example of a constructive critique. It is thorough and gives the authors some very specific points to consider. The length of the critique is not highly correlated with the publication decision. In fact, some reviewers write very short critiques for the manuscripts they dislike the most and write far more extensive critiques for manuscripts they see as potentially publishable.

Choosing Reviewers

The editor will normally keep a list of reviewers he or she respects for their own work. The editor will also maintain a list of those currently evaluating manuscripts and how many manuscripts each person has done during the year. Thus, a particular reviewer may not be chosen to review a manuscript because he/she either has already reviewed many manuscripts recently or is currently reviewing one.

Typically, the editor sends the manuscript to scholars who are experts in the topics addressed in the manuscript. For instance, if a manuscript uses a particular measuring instrument to study marital satisfaction, the editor is likely to send the manuscript to the person who developed the instrument and to another with expertise in marital satisfaction. Another way editors may select reviewers is by examining a manuscript's reference list. If certain authors tend to predominate and are available for reviewing, they are likely to be selected. After initially skimming the manuscript, the editor will check the availability of appropriate reviewers, often sending an abstract for the potential reviewer's consideration.

After the editor has had some experience with his/her reviewers, he/she knows some typical response patterns—who is detail oriented and who is not; who will give devastatingly negative reviews and who will focus on positive features of a manuscript; who responds quickly and who drags out the reviewing process. Thus, when an editor makes a decision about a reviewer, he or she is not simply choosing a person with experience in a particular area, but considering a number of other relevant factors as well.

Becoming a Reviewer

If you want to become a reviewer yourself, there are three general routes to accomplishing this: (1) being recommended by another scholar who is a reviewer, a colleague of the editor, or on the journal's editorial board; (2) becoming visible to the editor through the quality of your work or other scholarly activities, such as publication of an insightful book review; or (3) volunteering your services and documenting your area(s) of expertise. The first two are the most common paths to becoming a reviewer. Producing consistently high quality reviews, conference papers, and scholarly articles gets notice and increases the chances of your being invited to serve on an editorial board.

Recommending Reviewers

Authors generally should not recommend reviewers for their own manuscripts unless a manuscript is clearly an unusual piece. Even then, you should do this with care because you do not want to appear to be telling the editor how to do his/her job, or to give the impression that you think only your friends or colleagues are capable of fairly evaluating the work. If you think the editor will have trouble finding people to evaluate the manuscript fairly, perhaps the best strategy is to say that you would be happy to recommend possible reviewers at the editor's request.

"Blind" Review

Blind review is an effort to keep the identity of the author hidden so the reviewer focuses on the manuscript rather than on who wrote it. That is the ideal. In reality, there are many so-called "blind" reviews in which the author's identity is known. This can happen because the author's programmatic research tends to cite his or her own previous research a great deal; because the reviewer knows and has discussed the research with the author or coauthor; because the area of research is limited to a few individuals; or because the author inadvertently mentions his or her university or leaves a blank space in the references where his or her name would fall. Blind reviewing is still the most popular method used, although some journals now give both authors and reviewers the option of blind or open reviews. Some reviewers wish anonymity for fear that a critical review will affect their chances of publication if the tables are ever reversed; others believe it is important for authors to know who is reviewing so they can be fully aware of the perspective the reviewer holds.

What Kind of Feedback Do Editors Provide?

Two types of feedback are common. In one the editor digests the reviews and writes a letter synthesizing what he/she feels are the important points—

along with the publication decision. The other approach involves copying and sending along reviewer comments verbatim and indicating which comments are to be given the most attention and which most influenced the publication decision. In addition, some editors send copies of the decision letter (without the author's name) to the reviewers so they are informed of the publication decision and/or the editor's expectations for revision. (See Appendix F for an example of a letter from an editor to an author.) Sometimes editors make sure each reviewer sees the comments of every other reviewer.

The editor will communicate only with the submitting author (normally the first author). It is the responsibility of the submitting author to keep his or her coauthors informed of any decisions regarding their manuscript.

Contacting the Editor About Disposition of a Manuscript
If you have not heard from the editor regarding your manuscript after three or four months, it is appropriate to ask *when* you can expect to have a decision. Be sure to refer to your manuscript by the identifying number assigned by the editor. Many editors prefer that you inquire by letter or email rather than by telephone. Because of the complexity of reviews and the often detailed nature of revision suggestions, it is not likely that the editor will convey the publication decision over the telephone. There is also a risk of misunderstanding, but a letter or email request about when a decision is expected is appropriate.

There are many reasons for delay in making decisions on manuscripts, but by far the most common is the inability of an editor to get a review back from a reviewer. When manuscripts are sent to reviewers, most editors will suggest sending the manuscript back if it cannot be reviewed by a certain date. Unfortunately, many scholars do not send them back even when they are too busy to make the deadline. In cases in which reviewers differ greatly in their evaluations, the editor may send the manuscript to a third reader. This also increases the time it takes to reach a decision. Availability of reviewers during certain times of the year can also delay reviewing and editing time. Finally, many decisions to be made by the editor are not clear-cut. Because of the many factors an editor weighs in coming to a decision—other articles submitted on the same topic, amount of work needed in revision, deadlines, experience of the author, likelihood that revision will be undertaken, and so on—a careful editorial letter and decision may also take some time.

If Your Manuscript Is Rejected

Eighty to 85 percent of the manuscripts submitted to communication journals are rejected. Below are some rejection rates reported by the National Communication Association on its website:

Communication Monographs, 1996–98 (82%)
Critical Studies in Mass Communication, 1996–98 (81.7%)
Journal of Applied Communication Research, 1997–1999 (83.9%)
Quarterly Journal of Speech, 1996–98 (78.3%)

Other journals in the field of communication report similar rates. These percentages are determined by counting the number of manuscripts submitted to a journal and comparing that to the number ultimately published—but this may not tell the entire story. Many authors, when asked to revise and resubmit their manuscripts, never do so. Those manuscripts fall in the nonacceptance pile, even though in reality no final decision was ever reached by the editor.

Most manuscripts are rejected because of problems detected by the editor and/or reviewers, but some that are technically "clean" are rejected because they may not address a large enough body of the journal's audience or because the editors and reviewers do not believe the article makes a sufficiently important contribution to the literature.

Editors are careful about saying "yes," "no," or "maybe." You generally can assume you still have a chance for publication unless there is a clear "no" in the editor's letter. If you are rejected by one journal, you still may be accepted by another. Pay careful attention to the recommendations made by reviewers and make whatever changes you think appropriate and possible, revamp for the new audience, and send the manuscript to another journal. What is inappropriate for one journal may be just what another editor is looking for. Although unlikely, there is a slight possibility you may get the same reviewer if you send the manuscript to another journal—another reason why revision is important. Remember also that different journals have different standards and different needs. If the rejection was made after a prompt and fair evaluation process, and reviewers have offered constructive comments, the review process served its purposes. This doesn't mean that you have to agree with the reviewers or editor; it doesn't mean that the editor and reviewers were "right" and you were "wrong"; and it doesn't mean that you don't do quality work. It means only that on this occasion, for these people, and for this specific journal, this work was judged less positively than other submissions.

The "Inappropriate" Review

A critical or negative review is not necessarily inappropriate if it includes observations that are constructive and that will improve the article. In many cases, the reviewers' comments are written so that editors can make either a positive or negative decision depending on how each comment is weighed. However, a review in which it is clear that the reviewer read only a portion of the manuscript instead of reading the entire manuscript carefully, or one that is totally insulting and includes no constructive comments, is inappropriate and unprofessional. Normally, an editor will not send these to an author, but it does happen. As the author, you may wish to contact the editor and request another review. The editor may or may not solicit another review but ultimately, the decision is the editor's—regardless of what the reviewers say.

Should you have documentable evidence of unprofessional behavior by an editor, such as publishing a manuscript that received two recommendations of rejection or not publishing one accepted by two reviewers, you should first discuss the matter with the editor. If it is not resolved to the your satisfaction, you may want to bring the issue to the publication chair or president of the association that made the appointment. The association may also have an ethics policy outlining procedures for dealing with such issues.

Summary of Author/Editor Expectations in the Review Process

Author	Editor
Expects the review process to take no longer than 3–4 months.	Expects authors to give him/her credit for conducting a prompt, thorough, and impartial review process.
Expects the manuscript to be evaluated by experts.	Expects his/her reviewers to meet deadlines unless they give advance notification.
Expects the manuscript to be evaluated fairly.	
Expects the editor to provide concrete reasons in writing for his/her publication decision.	

THE REVISION AND RESUBMISSION PROCESS

The Meaning of Revise and Resubmit

The recommendation to revise and resubmit may be given for several different reasons: The manuscript may be technically correct but poorly written; the editor may want a manuscript like yours and is willing to work with you to get it ready for publication; the manuscript is a potentially good one, but a lack of clarity in some parts of it makes it difficult to tell. Only in very rare cases is a manuscript published without some kind of revision. The "revise and resubmit" letter essentially says, "I'd like to see more before making a decision." This is not a commitment to publish your manuscript, but if an editor asks for a second or third revision, it usually means he or she is seriously hoping the manuscript can be published. Still, there are a few occasions when a manuscript is rejected even after several revisions.

It is inappropriate to withdraw a manuscript in the midst of a multiple revision process. The editor and reviewers have invested time and effort toward publishing your manuscript and do not want their work to be the basis of a submission to another journal—unless, of course, they have formally rejected the manuscript.

Understanding What the Editor Wants You to Do

An editor might send a "revise and resubmit" letter that you find ambiguous. Perhaps the editor is not clear in his or her own mind what he or she wants done; perhaps the editor does not want to be too precise in making prescriptions for change because such advice would detract from general, more abstract issues that pervade the manuscript. Nevertheless, if you do not understand what is being requested of you, you should contact the editor by email to ask for clarification, explaining what you intended in writing the passage.

If the editor sends two reviewer critiques and does not specify which changes are to be made, you should make those you believe have merit and provide reasons why you did not make other changes.

Making Revisions Suggested by the Editor

You are under no obligation to make revisions. Taking such a position, however, may affect your chances for acceptance. If you can build a strong case and convince the editor that there are good reasons for not making the changes, your manuscript may be accepted without revision. The usual case involves compromise—some changes are made as recommended, some are made in slightly different ways than originally suggested, and some requested changes are not made at all.

Submitting the Revision

When returning the revised manuscript to the editor, your package should include (1) a brief cover letter with the manuscript's identification number; (2) a statement of which recommended changes were made, how they were made, and on what pages; (3) a statement of which recommended changes were not made and why (reviewers do make mistakes and have biases, so you should not feel obligated to make a particular change if you feel there are good reasons not to—editors can and have been persuaded by well-reasoned arguments); and (4) a statement indicating your perception of how certain recommendations or perhaps all recommendations have strengthened the manuscript. Because publication is a negotiated process, a comment like this simply acknowledges that you are doing your part.

Deadlines for Resubmission

Some editors specify a deadline for resubmission, but others do not. Revising and resubmitting as quickly as possible means that issues surrounding your manuscript will be fresh and salient for both you and the reviewers of your manuscript. Furthermore, if you wait too long, the editor who asked you to revise and resubmit may be replaced or fill up his or her remaining issues with other accepted articles. This would mean you would have to start the editorial process over again because incoming editors are under no obligation to accept manuscripts from a previous editorship. Editors are typically appointed by an association or publisher for a limited term. In the communication field, the most common term is three years. It may be close to a year before your article actually appears in the journal after the time it is accepted—another reason for doing revisions as quickly as possible. Editors often express surprise by the number of "revise and resubmit" manuscripts that are never returned. There is much to be said for persistence in the publishing process. Authors who are willing to undertake revisions and resubmit have a much better chance of eventual acceptance than the critical comments of reviewers might suggest!

Seeing Your Article in Print

After looking through the article and accepting a manuscript for publication, the editor will determine when it will be published. The time it takes from acceptance to publication varies from journal to journal and from editor to editor. There is almost always some delay, and it is not unusual to wait a year before seeing your article in print. There are a number of reasons for this: Other articles may have been accepted before yours and assumed a higher publication priority; space available in a particular issue (which is often contractual) may not match the length of your article—for example, your article is 25 pages long and there are only 17 pages left to fill in the issue; or your article may be held for a special issue devoted to a particular theme. For similar reasons, your article could be published quickly—few articles in a new editorship may have been accepted prior to yours; your article may exactly match the length needed to fill an issue and no article accepted before yours does; or an appropriate theme issue may be scheduled soon after your article was accepted.

Going to Press

After a manuscript is accepted, the editor or assistant will prepare it for the printer. He or she may edit the manuscript to fit the journal's style, to eliminate what he or she sees as redundancy, or to clean up the writing. Editors differ in how much they will work over a manuscript. If revisions are substantial, the editor will usually consult the author to make sure the changes are acceptable.

Once all articles for a given issue are deemed editorially "ready," the editor will send them to the printer, who will prepare typeset proofs for the author and editor to proofread. (With desktop publishing, typesetting may be done by the editorial office or by the publisher or printer). This version of the article is the last contact the author will have with his or her article prior to printing. Proofs are usually sent to the author just prior to printing, thus the demanded turnaround time is often very short (about 48 hours). Proofs may be returned to the editor or to the publisher/printer, depending on who did the typesetting and will do the corrections.

The author should read proofs with attention to detail and make needed corrections using accepted proofreader symbols (see Appendix D). At this stage, the author should make only those corrections that are absolutely necessary for clarity and precision. It is important to read the entire proof to avoid having errors appear in the published article. Be careful not to skim too quickly and miss errors (e.g., in quotes, references, or in entire lines of text being omitted). Check for correspondence between citations in the manuscript and those in the reference list. Be aware that errors sometimes crop up in tables, figures, and statistical data and those should be closely scrutinized for completeness, accuracy, and visual clarity.

Proofing and correction procedures are changing rapidly as more and more journals adopt on-line submission and editing. You should always check a publication's website for the latest guidelines and instructions from the editor.

Determining the Order of Articles in an Issue
The editor creates an order for the journal's table of contents. Ordering is done in different ways by different editors. Some editors highlight a particular article (a "lead" article); others publish articles in order of acceptance; some use an alphabetical scheme; and others try to create a particular thematic cluster or diversity. Authors should not be too concerned about where in an issue their article appears.

Copyright
Authors are often asked to sign forms that protect the journal against any improprieties by the author and that protect the author against unwarranted use of his or her article after it appears in the journal. Each journal differs in the specific language. See Appendix E for an example of a copyright form.

Reprints
In most cases, authors will receive at least one extra copy of the journal issue that contains their article. Many journals also offer authors the opportunity to order reprints of their article.

Feedback From You to the Editor
Editors, rightly or wrongly, perceive themselves as having a difficult job. When you consider that 80–85% of the letters an editor writes are letters of rejection, the basis for these feelings is evident. Editors also receive their share of letters critical of the way some aspect of the process was conducted. Authors should not hesitate to write letters expressing positive perceptions or making suggestions for improvement. Authors whose manuscripts have been rejected for publication have been known to compliment the editor on the way the process was conducted.

Although the editorial process has been our primary focus, the end product (the journal itself) also may be the target of positive and negative feedback for the editor. In general, everyone involved in producing and reading a scholarly journal has an investment in its quality and should not hesitate to provide constructive feedback. Authors whose manuscripts have been accepted will sometimes acknowledge the assistance of anonymous reviewers who made suggestions that substantially improved the manuscript. This is entirely appropriate if the editor and journal permits such acknowledgments, but some do not.

Summary of Author/Editor Expectations
in the Revision and Resubmission Process

Author

Expects a clear indication from the editor of which revisions are required and which are just recommended.

Expects the editor to enter the revision process in the spirit of compromise.

Expects the editor to communicate in a professional manner.

Expects the editor to provide guidance and information necessary to complete the publication process after the manuscript is accepted.

Editor

Expects the author to make the requested revisions or indicate why they were not made.

Expects author to enter the revision process in the spirit of compromise.

Expects the revision to be done within the timeframe the editor specifies.

Expects the author to work quickly and accurately in returning final copy, proofs, and copyright forms necessary for publication.

APPENDIX A

EXAMPLE OF
AUTHOR COVER LETTER

January 12, 2003

JANE Q. EDITOR
Journal of _____
State University of Wherever
Department of Communication Studies
Anywhere, USA

Dear Dr. _____:

Enclosed you will find four copies of a manuscript entitled, "An Analysis of Comforting Messages Communicated to Owners of Recently Deceased Pets" which my coauthor and I would like to submit to the *Journal of* _____ for review and possible publication.

I look forward to hearing from you.

Sincerely,

John Q. Author
mailing address
phone number
email address

APPENDIX B

EXAMPLE OF
MANUSCRIPT REVIEW FORM

Journal of _____
Manuscript Review Form

MSTitle: _____

MS # _____ Reviewer: _____

Signature: _____

Recommendation (check one):

_____Publish as is
_____Publish with minor revisions indicated below
_____Publish with major revisions indicated below
_____Revise and resubmit
_____Submit to another journal, e.g.,
_____Reject

Manuscript Rating (5 = average quality):

Overall Impression of Quality   Importance of the Researchable Idea
Low 1 2 3 4 5 6 7 8 9 High   Low 1 2 3 4 5 6 7 8 9 High

Methodology   Style
Unclear 1 2 3 4 5 6 7 8 9 Clear   Weak 1 2 3 4 5 6 7 8 9 Strong

Comments to the Author:
(Please indicate on a separate sheet your detailed and candid opinion regarding this manuscript.)

Return to:
Dr. John Q. Editor
Dept of Communication
General University
Anywhere, USA

APPENDIX C

EXAMPLE OF A CONSTRUCTIVE CRITIQUE

I am generally favorably disposed to the publication of manuscript #2043 although there are some specific and, I believe, serious issues that the authors must address before I could recommend publication. These issues are outlined below. If the editor concurs with me, I will be happy to review a revised version of this manuscript for publication in _____ . I strongly encourage the authors to revise.

Before presenting the negative criticisms, let me mention, briefly, the positive attributes of this manuscript. It is well-written and reflects considerable knowledge of the relevant literature. The phenomena explored are basic to the field of communication, although perhaps not too flashy. By and large, the theorizing is tightly reasoned (exceptions noted below). The methodological criticisms of previous literature, particularly the factor analytic studies, reflect some sophistication. All in all it is a good paper, however, it is marred by weaknesses that require revision.

1. The definitions of the basic variables in the model are a bit loose. For instance, P (participation) is "each person's share of the *activity* and *talking* in the group" (p. 2). "Activity" is hardly a precise term. (Is nonverbal activity included or just verbal activity?) Operationally, the authors permit anything from the number of "social acts" to total duration of talk, to number of words/discussions among peer reports of talkativeness as indices of P. This appears to be pretty fuzzy. It could be tidied up by reporting the relatively strong correlations that exist in the literature among objective measures of verbal output. I do not know how self- or peer reports correlated with these objective measures. Perhaps the authors do. At any rate, the operational indicators of P need to be shown to represent a single conceptual domain with empirical evidence.

Similar problems plague the E (evaluation) variable. Here the authors define E in terms of an individual's "positive or negative feelings toward people or their behavior" (p. 2). Feelings about what? Their actions? Their personalities? Their abilities? Their contributions? It seems to me that those do not present a single conceptual domain. If not, then there exists a set of curves (as in Fig. 3) with the same P as the x-axis and different Es as the y-axis. If so, does the observer have to make all the Es and Ps fit the equilibrium points? What about potential trade-offs between types of evaluation? Might I increase my evaluation of someone's abilities and decrease personal liking to bring both Es into equilibrium? If the authors cannot demonstrate the conceptual and empirical coherence of the E dimension, these are some of the questions they should address, at least in footnote format.

2. There appears to be an inconsistency in the authors' use of evidence. They argue that low or zero correlations should be expected in factor analytic studies of the relationship between P and E. This is a reasonable conclusion given Figure 3. But if this is true, why did the studies reported on pp 7–10 indicate a positive linear relationship? If I could run a regression line through either Figures 2 or 3, I should get a near zero or negative beta coefficient. Why, then, did all those studies reveal a moderately strong positive relationship? This apparent contradiction needs to be resolved.

I believe that there is an easy resolution, if one will grant that the P-axis has a probability distribution laid on it such that the extreme ends of the axis are very far out on the tails of this distribution. In effect, while we have words to describe people who are so talkative as to be negatively evaluated (Figure 2), we simply do not find *people* who fit those descriptions very often. As a consequence, we find few data points in the extreme ends of the P-axis, and its middle range (15%–55% perhaps) defines the shape of the regression line of E regressed on P. The authors might consider this explanation of the apparent contradiction noted above. Should they adopt it, they should consider what it might do to the practical significance of their claims.

3. The rationale and evidence supporting the dynamic equilibrium portion of the theory are weak. The hypothesis that individuals attempt to force others to fit their own view of the P-E relationship is an intriguing one—which I find to be plausible. On the other hand, the plausibility of that such improvement might take—one theoretical and one empirical. The theoretical improvement centers on a gap in the current formulation. On p. 17 the authors suggest that the mechanism, causing observers to seek equilibrium between actual P and actual E and expected versions of both is "a process similar to those posited by dissonance or balance theory [sic]. "On p. 19 they argue that departures from the expected P-E curve are "motivating." What is the nature of this motivation? If such departures are simply dissonance producing, the authors have inherited a large body of literature, replete with controversies, addressing the presence, absence or contingent factors influencing dissonance reduction. I can't figure out how the balance theory option would fit in. Perhaps the authors could enlighten me. Regardless, my point is that there is a gap in theoretical coverage that demands attention. I can see no reason to accept an equilibrium hypothesis unless the authors can give me a reason for accepting equilibrium to exist.

The empirical move that the authors might make to strengthen this section is quite direct. They currently have very little data to support the equilibrium component of their theory. Either they need to get more from reviews of their literature or amplify more on what they have (cited on p. 21 but blanked out in my copy), or report the results of a pilot test (this is the best option; a full-fledged study doesn't seem necessary if the other changes mentioned above are undertaken) or all three.

As I noted at the beginning of my critique, I am positively disposed toward this piece. I have raised no objection that I believe cannot be overcome by the authors in some fashion. I am even willing to hear counterarguments on my criticism, but until my objections are circumvented in some fashion I am unwilling to recommend publication.

PS: I have made some detailed comments in the margins of the manuscript. Please forward these to the authors. They cover stylistic and minor substantive issues that have not been addressed in my review.

APPENDIX D

STANDARD PROOFREADER MARKS

PROOFREADERS MARKS*

Margin Mark	Mark in Typeset Text

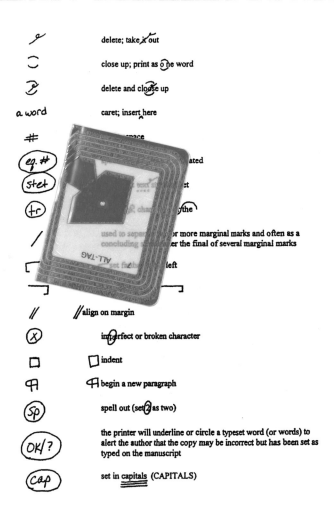

delete; take it out

close up; print as one word

delete and close up

a word — caret; insert here

— ...pace

eq. # — ...ated

stet — ...ct

tr — ...the

/ — used to separate... or more marginal marks and often as a concluding... er the final of several marginal marks

⌐ — ...left

// — // align on margin

Ⓧ — imperfect or broken character

☐ — ☐ indent

¶ — ¶ begin a new paragraph

sp — spell out (set 2 as two)

OK/? — the printer will underline or circle a typeset word (or words) to alert the author that the copy may be incorrect but has been set as typed on the manuscript

cap — set in capitals (CAPITALS)

---

* Authors, editors, and printers use proofreaders marks to indicate changes on printed proofs. Theses standard marks are used in pairs, one in the text where the change is to be made and one in the margin closest to the change.

Proofreaders Marks, continued

Margin Mark	Mark in Typeset Text

lc (circled) — set in lowercase (lowercase)

ital (circled) — set in italic (*italic*)

rom (circled) — set in <u>roman</u> (roman)

bf (circled) — set in boldface (**boldface**)

/=/ — insert hyphen (self imposed)

∨ — superscript ($\forall$ as in χ^2)

∧ — subscript ($\wedge$ as in H_2O)

◊ — centered (◊ for a centered dot in $p \cdot q$)

⩘ — insert comma (yes whereas)

⩗ — insert apostrophe (editors)

⊙ — insert period (end Then)

; — insert semicolon (this in)

: — insert colon (Tests Part 1)

⩗/⩗ — insert quotation marks (less than comparative)

(/) — insert parentheses (only two)

[/] — insert brackets (these 12 subjects)

APPENDIX E

EXAMPLE OF A TYPICAL JOURNAL
ASSIGNMENT OF COPYRIGHT FORM

Human Communication Research
Copyright Assignment Form

Sponsor: International Communication Assn.

Oxford University Press
Journals Department
2001 Evans Road
Cary, NC 27513, USA

Your paper has been accepted for publication in *Human Communication Research* (the Journal). **Please Read this Agreement carefully, sign where appropriate, and return the form to the journal Editor (at the address below).** Please note that all authors must sign the Agreement before your submission can be published. You may photocopy the form to distribute to co-authors.

Assignment of Copyright

TitleofArticle _____

To be completed by the copyright holder:
I attest that I am the author of this material and that it is an original work not previously published in whole or substantial part; that it is free of plagiarism; and that I have exercised reasonable care to ensure that the material is not inaccurate, libelous, or obscene and that it does not infringe on any copyright, right of privacy, or other right of any third party.

I hereby assign to the International Communication Association the copyright present and future in the above-named article for the legal term of the copyright including all renewals or extensions in all languages throughout the world. The granting of copyright entitles the International Communication Association to publish the material in the Journal and to reproduce the article in any form or medium now or hereafter known throughout the world.

Notwithstanding this grant of rights, I retain the right to use the work I have submitted, without charges, in other publications written or edited by myself, provided that I acknowledge the Journal as the original place of publication and that the Publisher, Oxford University Press, is notified of any prepublication (at the address above). I also retain the right to mount my article on my own personal World Wide Web home page and/or that of my employer's, provided that I (i) acknowledge the Journal as the original place of publication and the International Communication Association as the copyright owner and (ii) provide electronic links from my article to the Publisher's home page for the Journal http://www.hcr.oupjournals.org/ and to the International Communication Association's Web site http://www.icahdg.org.

If I am an employee of the US Government submitting a work of the US Government, insofar as I am able within the constraints of national law, I hereby assign the rights of the above-named article to the International Communication Association, according to the terms above.

_____   _____
Signature   Print Name

_____
Date

Please return this signed form to Editor, *Human Communication Research*, Department of Communication, General University, Anywhere, USA

43

APPENDIX F

EXAMPLES OF LETTERS OF ACCEPTANCE, REJECTION, AND REVISE/RESUBMIT

(Acceptance Letter)

Date _____

Dear Dr. _____:

The purpose of this letter is to formally accept your manuscript entitled

_____

The reviewers went through the revision and made certain minor suggestions that I have completed on the manuscript. I've enclosed a copy of the final version that was sent to the publisher for your perusal. Assuming the changes are acceptable, you should see the article in the journal in a future issue (probably the October issue).

I have enclosed a copyright release form which you'll need to sign and return to the publisher as soon as possible. They can't go further with the manuscript until they have it in their hands.

I do want to thank you for letting us have this piece. Your contribution is an important one that will, I believe, be well received by the field.

If you have any questions, please don't hesitate to get in touch with me.

Best wishes,

Jane Q. Editor

(Rejection Letter)

Date:_____

Dear Dr._____:

We now have reviews of your manuscript entitled _____
_____, which you
submitted to the journal in September of this year.

Regrettably, the reviews were not positive about the manuscript.
Neither reviewer thought the piece suitable for publication in this
journal. I have enclosed copies of the reviews with this letter for your
information. Looking over the reviews and your manuscript, I find that
I must agree with the reviewers' recommendation not to publish this
piece. The major issues seem to be two: (1) methodological concerns
that raise questions about the validity of your claim, and (2) substantive
issues that led both reviewers to ask "so what?" in their remarks.

I have found that the single toughest task I face as an editor is telling
people that work they've obviously labored over isn't going to be
published. I hope that the reviews are helpful in both your future
scholarship and in finding a final home for this manuscript.

I do want to thank you for letting us look at the piece and express the
hope that in the future you'll again think of this journal as an outlet for
the best of your scholarship.

Best wishes,

John Q. Editor

(Revise/Resubmit Letter)

Date:_____

Dear Dr. _____:

We now have reviews of your manuscript entitled:

_____

_____, which you
submitted to the journal in July.

The reviews of the piece were mixed. One reviewer thought the
piece should be published with minor revisions; the other
thought substantial revisions would be necessary and recommended that the piece be returned to you for those changes and
then reconsidered. I've enclosed copies of both reviews with this
letter.

Looking over the reviews and the manuscript I tend to agree with
the second reviewer. I'd like to see a revision of the manuscript.
The major concerns are:

(1) a more succinct introduction that highlights more directly the
    hypothesis being tested.
(2) a more thorough discussion of the methods and results
    emphasizing issues such as reliability, how the classes were
    actually taught, issues of control, and the reasons for choosing
    regression over other procedures that might seem more
    appropriate initially (e.g., a discriminant analysis).
(3) the discussion section needs to include some implications for
    the classroom.

The reviewers were also in agreement that the writing needs
improvement. Please make sure you carefully proof any revision
you submit.
If you decide to submit a revision, here are the editorial guidelines.

(1) You understand that this is not an acceptance. The revision
    will be circulated to members of the editorial board for

another review. Only after this review will a final decision be made about the manuscript's acceptance.

(2) For purposes of maintaining a stream of manuscripts, I will need the revision in my hands within six weeks of your receiving this letter. If there is a problem with this deadline, please let me know.

(3)   As much as possible, please try to ensure that the revision deals directly with the reviewers' suggestions. Please enclose with the revision a letter detailing, point-by-point, the modifications you made vis-à-vis the reviewers' suggestions.

I do hope you'll consider a revision of the piece.

Whatever you do decide, I want to thank you for letting us look at the piece. And, I hope that in the future you'll again think of the journal as an outlet for the best of your scholarly work.

Best wishes,

John Q. Editor

APPENDIX G

ICA PUBLICATION POLICIES
AND PROCEDURES MANUAL

ICA Publication Policies and Procedures
(adopted by the ICA Board of Directors, July 2002)

GENERAL PUBLICATION POLICIES

The ICA publication program shall be operated in support of the basic purposes of the Association. As outlined in Article II of the ICA Bylaws, the Association is committed to advancing the scholarly study of human communication and facilitating the implementation of such study to the maximum benefit to humankind. Toward that end, the Association sustains a commitment to a program of scholarly publication and, in Article IV, Section 3, of the Bylaws, empowers the Board of Directors to approve the appointment of editors of its publications.

Article IX, Section 2(f), of the Association Bylaws provides for a Publications Committee to advise the Board of Directors in matters relevant to the Association's publication program. The specific responsibilities of the Board of Directors regarding oversight of the publication program are outlined in the four sections of Article X of the

Bylaws:

SECTION 1. The Association engages in the preparation, production, sale, and distribution of such occasional or regular scholarly publications as the Board of Directors shall determine.

SECTION 2. The Board of Directors shall arrange for the preparation and publishing of the Association's scholarly publications and shall determine the financial and organizational terms of the agreement.

SECTION 3. No regular publication shall be discontinued nor a regular publication added to the program without two-thirds majority of the entire Board of Directors approving such action.

SECTION 4. The editors of ICA publications are to be selected under procedures established by the ICA Board of Directors.

This publication manual serves to facilitate the execution of the Board's duties and provides specific procedures for fulfilling these responsibilities.

The authority of the Publications Committee and the Board of Directors is applicable to all ICA scholarly publishing activities. Any change in the statements regulating publication policies, procedures, or practices shall be reviewed and recommended by the Publication Committee and approved by the Board of Directors.

Ownership of Copyright

In all contracts negotiated with publishers, copyright shall be retained by ICA, unless ICA's Board of Directors approves other arrangements with authors and publishers in advance.

Permission to Reprint

Permission to reproduce material published by ICA for scholarly, not-for-profit purposes, and any charges associated therewith, should be at the discretion of the Executive Director.

Joint Publications

ICA may engage in cooperative publication efforts with other associations, organizations, and commercial or university presses when (1) it is to the financial advantage of ICA to do so and/or (2) it benefits the credibility or distribution of the publication. However, under no circumstances shall ICA enter into agreements whereby the Association loses editorial control of a publication's content.

Periodic Review

Specific policies and procedures for all ICA publications will be prepared in accordance with the general publication policies of the Association and will be reviewed periodically by the Publications Committee and always prior to the renewal of a commercial publication contract or formal agreement of joint publication with another professional entity.

PUBLICATIONS COMMITTEE

As outlined in Article IX, Section 2(f), of the ICA Bylaws, the Publications Committee acts as an agent of the Board of Directors and is responsible to it. The Publications Committee Chair, on behalf of the Committee, shall submit formal written reports to the semiannual Board meetings.

The Publications Committee shall consist of three members who serve for staggered three-year terms. Each ICA President shall appoint one new member to the Committee; the senior member shall serve as Chair. The Publications Committee shall monitor and make recommendations concerning the publication needs of the membership and the adequacy of existing publications to fill those needs. The Committee shall also nominate editors for all official ICA scholarly publications.

The Publications Committee shall convene regularly at the Association's annual convention. Time, place, and agenda of the meeting shall be announced by the Publications Committee Chair in the *ICA Newsletter* published immediately prior to each convention. ICA members shall be encouraged to attend, thus ensuring broad-based input from all areas and interests across the Association.

SERIAL PUBLICATIONS

The Association currently publishes four serials: *Human Communication Research, Journal of Communication, Communication Theory,* and *Communication Yearbook.*

Editorial Policies

Editorial policies of ICA's serials are determined by the Association through the policies of its Board of Directors. Editorial policies are not controlled by individual editorial decisions.

If an editor wishes to redirect the editorial policy of a particular journal, he or she must submit a written petition to the Publications Committee for consideration.

Editorial policy concerns the content, focus, and substance of the manuscripts published and usually does not concern procedures followed in manuscript review and evaluation. More specific editorial guidelines are included in the second part of this document. Current policies of the four serials follow:

Human Communication Research
Human Communication Research is devoted to advancing knowledge and understanding about human symbolic activities. Manuscripts reporting original research, methodologies relevant to the study of human communication, critical syntheses of research, and theoretical and philosophical perspectives on human communicative activity are encouraged. The journal maintains a broad behavioral and social scientific focus but reflects no particular methodological or substantive bias.

Journal of Communication
The *Journal of Communication* publishes articles and book reviews that examine a broad range of issues in communication theory, research, practice, and policy. Because the *Journal* seeks to be a general forum for communication scholarship, ICA is especially interested in research whose significance crosses disciplinary and subfield boundaries.

Communication Theory
Communication Theory publishes research articles, theoretical essays, and reviews on topics of broad theoretical interest from across the range of communication studies. Essays, regardless of topic or methodological approach, must make a significant contribution to communication theory. *Communication Theory* recognizes that approaches to theory development and explication are diverse. No single approach or set of approaches is privileged.

Communication Yearbook

Communication Yearbook publishes reviews of the literature in each of the areas represented by the divisions and interest groups of the ICA. In consultation with representatives of the ICA divisions, the editor chooses topics to be reviewed on a yearly basis and commissions reviewers. The reviews will provide syntheses of the available literature and critical assessment of their strengths and weaknesses.

Financial Support

ICA provides financial assistance to the editorial offices of official Association publications in order to sustain the editorial integrity of the publication program and to ensure that the financial limitations of prospective host institutions do not weaken the pool of potential editors.

The amount of university support shall be determined annually in the ICA budgeting process based on the budget needs submitted by each editor. Editors are expected to obtain some support from their universities during their editorships, with ICA supplementing that support as needed. These amounts are intended to help offset departmental and university support for the journal and are not expected to fully compensate the editor or host institution for costs incurred.

In the case of new publications, start-up funds may be provided to enable these publications to compete adequately in the marketplace. Once publications are firmly established in the field, the amount of annual funding provided to support editorial operations beyond the base provision shall be reduced accordingly.

Requests for budgets in excess of the limits established for each publication may be submitted, but they will be approved only in extraordinary circumstances and with consideration to the overall financial health of the Association.

Appointment of Editors

Editors of all ICA serial publications and commissioned books and monographs shall be nominated by the Publications Committee and appointed to three-year terms by the Board of Directors. The Publications Committee, as a regular part of its responsibilities, shall periodically review the length of editorial terms.

Editors of ICA publications should reflect the diversity of the Association in interest, gender, ethnicity, and national origin.

The Publications Committee will review nominations for editors and submit a recommendation to the Board of Directors, along with documentation to support the nomination. The Board of Directors will consider the Committee's nomination and either appoint the Committee's choice, appoint another nominee, or ask the Committee to continue its search.

The Executive Director serves as Editor of the *ICA Newsletter*. Although the Publications Committee maintains oversight of the *ICA Newsletter,* a separate Newsletter Committee governs routine procedures related to its production.

No person should hold more than one editorial position within the Association at any one time, nor be permitted to succeed herself/ himself in the editorial post. However, in the event of extraordinary circumstances that merit special consideration, the Board of Directors may suspend these policy restrictions by a two-thirds vote of its members.

Editors must be members of the International Communication Association at the time of their nomination, appointment, and throughout their editorial terms.

Editors are expected to attend the annual ICA convention and to participate in programs or panels relevant to their editorial tasks. Attendance at the annual meeting facilitates fulfillment of the editor's responsibility to meet with potential authors and encourage manuscript submission. Such attendance is seen as integral to the editor's own professional development and, hence, is not funded by ICA.

Editors are responsible for familiarizing themselves thoroughly with ICA Publication Policies and Procedures and abiding by them.

Removal of Editors From Office

In the event that an editor is jeopardizing the reputation of the publication and/or the Association by failure to adhere to policies, procedures, or established schedules, the Executive Committee, acting on behalf of the Board of Directors and with the advice and recommendation of the Publications Committee, may remove an editor from office and appoint a replacement editor for the remainder of the editorial term or a specified time period not to exceed the remainder plus one full term. The Executive Committee is empowered to make substitute editorial appointments in the event of emergency, such as incapacity of an editor while in office. Such appointments are made with the advice and recommendation of the Publications Committee and should be accompanied by a specific set of arrangements for transferring editorial responsibility and support functions.

Editorial Responsibilities

Editorial Board

Each editor has sole responsibility for structuring, soliciting, and choosing his or her editorial review board. Editorial board members should reflect the diversity of submissions to the journal, the various constituencies of ICA, and the quality of judgment necessary to insure the publication of excellent scholarship.

Publication Standards

Standards and procedures for the review of manuscripts are at the discretion of the editor. Submissions should be reviewed by experts in the field and reviews completed within 12 weeks of submission.

Social Science Citation Index

Editors should be mindful of the annual rankings of ICA serials in the Social Science Citation Index and uphold the highest standards for scholarship published in ICA journals in a continual effort to better our standings.

Publication Decisions

The acceptance or rejection of individual manuscripts is at the sole discretion of the editor. Input from members of the editorial board is advisory and editors may make decisions consistent with that advice. Editors may not place final decisions regarding acceptance or rejection in the hands of individual board members, associate editors, or any other group.

Contractual Agreements

Editors are responsible for familiarizing themselves with all aspects of contracts governing their journal and for understanding these contractual agreements.

To assure timely distribution of the publication and to protect the integrity and reputation of ICA's publication program, editors must abide by publication schedules established by ICA headquarters and production departments of commercial publishers with whom ICA has contracted.

Editors may not exceed contractual page allocations or budget limitations established by the Association or publisher. Editors should process submissions in a manner that assures timely publication of articles.

Publication Design

Editors may not change the graphic layout or structural features of journals without the written approval of the Publications Committee. Requests for changes in cover color/art, graphic layout, content headings, type size/format, or other production characteristics must be submitted to, and approved by, the Publications Committee before any changes can be implemented by ICA headquarters or a commercial publisher responsible for the production of an official ICA scholarly publication.

Publication Style
The ICA Board of Directors has directed that the editorial style of all ICA scholarly publications be governed by the latest edition of the *Publication Manual of the American Psychological Association.* It is the responsibility of the editorial office to see that each manuscript follows APA style.
Transition Between Editors
Incoming Editors are obliged to publish any papers formally accepted by the previous Editor; however, the Outgoing Editor should aim to transfer no more than two issues' worth of formally accepted papers to the Incoming Editor.

Reports by the Editor
Annual report. Each editor is expected to submit an annual report to the Publications Committee and the Board of Directors that may include any statements or recommendations that the editor chooses to bring before the Board, but must include the following:
    1. Summary of demographic characteristics of manuscript authors to include first author's gender, nationality of institution, and topic of article, as well as information on whether manuscript were accepted, returned for revision, or rejected for each of these categories.
    2. Summary of intellectual categories (e.g., cultural study, theoretical essay, experimental investigation or other designated categories appropriate to the publication) represented by the manuscripts submitted and published.
    3. Summary of review process including (a) number of manuscripts received, (b) time required for editorial decisions, (c) time between acceptance and publication, (d) number of revisions submitted for publication, (e) overall acceptance rate.

Financial report. Editors are required to submit detailed annual financial reports describing and justifying the use of ICA funds from the previous fiscal year. This report should accompany the request for funding for the coming fiscal year. This report must include a complete listing of specific disbursements (actual and projected) of ICA funds and a cover letter from the department chairperson (or financial officer) testifying to the accuracy of the accounting. ICA reserves the right to conduct an audit of the account to be certain that its monies are being spent to advance ICA's publication agenda.

ETHICAL STANDARDS

All manuscripts submitted to ICA publications must be *original* works that (a) credit all authors, (b) acknowledge sources and supporting material, and (c) identify previous publication of the manuscript in an earlier form. The place, time, and form of the previous publication, and whether the present material duplicates or is substantially different than the earlier presentation, must be made explicit in a cover letter accompanying the manuscript submission. ICA does not publish articles that have been previously published in substantially the same form.

Any manuscript submitted to an ICA publication must not be simultaneously considered by another publication. If extraordinary circumstances call for simultaneous submission, the ICA editor should be informed by the author(s). Decisions regarding the originality of and/or appropriateness of a submitted manuscript will be rendered by the editor. Evidence of alleged misconduct or ethical violations will be reported to the Publications Committee.

The editorial office will provide no information regarding the status of a submission to anyone other than the author (or a person the author designates in writing) of a manuscript, book review, or other material submitted to ICA for publication.

RECOGNITION OF EDITORS

The Association shall reward editors' generous donation of time and expertise with appropriate forms of recognition.

ADOPTION OR CREATION OF SERIAL PUBLICATIONS

All proposals for adoption of an existing journal or creation of a new scholarly publication shall be submitted to the Publications Committee for review, evaluation, and recommendation.

PUBLICATION CONTRACTS: SOLICITATION AND NEGOTIATION

The Executive Director shall solicit and negotiate all ICA publication contracts for consideration and approval by the Board of Directors.

BOOKS AND MONOGRAPHS

General Policies

The Publications Committee is responsible for the nomination of authors and editors of any nonserial ICA-sponsored books and monographs, with final appointments the responsibility of the Board of Directors. For an edited volume, the Publications Committee nominates and the Board of Directors appoints only the general editor. The editor has full authority to name all authors, associate editors, and other personnel needed to assist in the development of the publication. Any editor of an ICA-sponsored monograph or book must be a member of the Association at the time of appointment and publication.

Specific ICA book and monograph procedures shall be devised on a case-by-case basis, depending on whether the work is to be published in-house or by a commercial publisher. For each publication produced in-house, all matters concerned with production are the responsibility of the Executive Director of the Association. These will be spelled out in a publication agreement document signed by the author or editor, Executive Director, and the President. For each publication handled by a commercial publisher, a publication agreement document will be developed cooperatively by the Executive Director, the nominated Editor or Author, and the repre-sentative official of the publishing company. The agreement shall then be submitted to the Executive Committee for review and approval and, if approved, signed on behalf of the Association by the Executive Director and the President.

ICA should not normally offer honoraria or royalties to authors for publications sponsored by the Association. However, ICA may provide partial reimbursement for out-of-pocket costs to the individual or department involved, not to exceed 75% of the royalties generated by the publication. Under special circumstances, the Executive Committee may approve requests for honoraria or royalties to authors.

The Executive Director shall provide an annual report to the Board of Directors on the marketing, inventory, and sales of all ICA books and monographs whose distribution is handled by the Association. A file copy of any publication authorized by ICA shall be deposited at ICA headquarters.

Specific responsibililites of authors/editors are outlined in the procedures section of this document.

PUBLICATIONS BY ICA UNITS

All publication activities, other than newsletter publication, shall be coordinated with the Publications Committee. The publication of any journal, monograph, or book bearing the name of ICA, one of its divisions or interest groups, or other ICA units must have prior approval of the Board of Directors, following consideration by the Publications Committee and its recommendation to the Board.

ICA divisions, interest groups, committees, and task forces are encouraged to use the *ICA Newsletter* as a medium of communication with their members, although allocated funds may be used for unit newsletters, if deemed necessary.

ENDORSEMENT OR SPONSORSHIP OF NON-ICA PUBLICATIONS

It is not the policy of ICA to endorse, sponsor, or support publications of any type that have been generated by initiatives outside the Association. Exceptions to this practice may be made upon the recommendation of the Publications Committee and approval by the Board of Directors. Nonpublication products that ICA is asked to endorse or market must be sent to ICA headquarters for evaluation by the Executive Director. Products recommended by the Executive Director to the Board of Directors for endorsement and/or marketing must be approved by the Board before endorsement or marketing may take place.

Prior to action by the Board of Directors, the President may appoint a task force to evaluate the quality of the product and its suitability for Association sponsorship or marketing.

REVISIONS OF ICA PUBLICATION POLICIES & PROCEDURES

The Publications Committee will review the content of this document at least annually and, where appropriate, recommend changes to the Board of Directors.

Changes may also be recommended at any time by the Executive Director, the Executive Committee, or any member of the Board. ICA headquarters will maintain this document on the ICA website and will regularly make its existence and availability known to the Association membership, as well as to members being considered for the editorship or authorship of an ICA publication.

Procedures Guide for ICA Editors

GENERAL PUBLICATION PROCEDURES

Editors of ICA scholarly publications are expected to operate within the guidelines adopted by the ICA Board of Directors as outlined in this ICA Publications Policy and Procedures Guide.

The Procedures Guide will provide information and define the process by which ICA's publication agenda is realized.

Nomination/Appointment of Editors

ICA's editors are nominated by the Publications Committee and appointed by the Board of Directors.

The Publications Committee encourages a wide breadth of qualified scholars to apply and seeks the advice of ICA's intellectual leaders in the recruitment process in an effort to appoint editors who reflect the diversity of the Association in interest, gender, and ethnicity.

The nomination and application procedure, determined by the Publications Committee, typically follows these steps:

1. An open call for nominations and applications is published in the *ICA Newsletter* (and other appropriate outlets) well in advance of the completion of the editor's term, usually around the mid-point of the second year of the three-year term.

2. The Publications Committee might also solicit editorial nominations from members of the journal's existing editorial board and/or may encourage division and interest group chairs to make the opening known to their members, who may then apply on an individual basis.

3. Current editors should encourage outstanding members of their editorial boards and/or frequent contributors to self-nominate for vacant editorships.
4. Nominations and applications are submitted to the Publications Committee Chair with the following supporting documentation:

a. Statement of nomination or application including a statement outlining the candidate's plans and goals and expressing a willingness to serve if appointed.

b. A current vita.

c. Letters of support from persons qualified to assess the candidate's ability to edit the publication in question.

d. Letter from the responsible university administrator stating that adequate host institutional support will be provided, including released time, editorial work space, support personnel, and financial contributions to ensure the successful operation of the editorial office.

The appointment process requires the Publications Committee to review nominations and applications and to make a recommendation to the Board of Directors. After consideration, the Board will either ratify the recommendation, appoint another nominee, or ask the Committee to continue its search.

Financial Support

Editors of each serial publication are expected to submit an annual budget by March 1 of each year as part of ICA's budget planning process (ICA operates on a October through September fiscal year). Editors may have access to budgets of previous/current editors as needed to formulate a budget request for the following year.

Editors are expected to obtain some support from their universities during their editorships, with ICA supplementing that support as needed. This support is intended to help offset departmental and university support for the journal and not to fully compensate the editor or host institution for costs incurred. The amount of annual university support from ICA shall be based on the budget needs submitted by each editor. Financial support of the journals is considered a reimbursement for actual expenses approved by the Board of Directors. Financial support for journal activities is not a grant or stipend to the editor or the editor's institution.

Budget requests should document the nature and extent of anticipated expenses (e.g., postage, copying, telephone, office supplies) in detail. The maximum reimbursement budgets for the editors are determined yearly by the Board of Directors upon recommendation by the Publications Committee in consultation with the Chair of the Finance Committee.

Budget limits are based on the understood functions of the various editorial offices. *Communication Yearbook* is guided by a more thematic model that invites scholarly contributions. Therefore, fewer unsolicited manuscripts must be processed through the stages of blind review and revision, as is the standard practice of *Human Communication Research* and *Communication Theory*. The *Journal of Communication* is significantly larger than *Human Communication Research* and *Communication Theory*, processes more manuscripts, and has a much more developed international orientation. Factors such as these and others peculiar to a each journal are considered in the budgeting process.

Formal reimbursement requests must be submitted by the editors before June 15 of each year. Requests for reimbursement must be accompanied by receipts or other appropriate documentation of expenses incurred. Failure to document expenditures could result in rejection of the reimbursement request. Funds may not be carried forward to the next fiscal year.

In extraordinary circumstances, requests exceeding the budgeted amounts will be considered by the Publications Committee and the Board of Directors; any such request must be accompanied by detailed justification.

Editorial Responsibilities and Procedures

As outlined in the policy section of this document, the editor has responsibility for appointing the editorial review board, establishing review standards and procedures, and accepting or rejecting indivudal manuscripts.

Editorial Assistants
It is also the editor's responsibility to determine the need for and specific responsibilities of editorial assistants, if any, and to hire one or more graduate students to fulfill these duties, outlining in detail the responsibilities of the position. The editor supervises the work of editorial assistant(s), but bears ultimate responsibility for the operation of the editorial office.

Editorial Review
Review procedures of ICA serial publications generally include (1) peer review, (2) multiple reviewers, (3) blind review, (4) written feedback to submitters from reviewers and editors, (5) sharing of reviews among reviewers, (6) acknowledgment of receipt of manuscripts, and (7) prompt response (within 12 weeks) to submissions. Variance from these practices should be undertaken only after consultation with the Publication Committee.

Division of Editorial Responsibilities

Editorial Office

- To bear ultimate responsibility for adherence to APA style, academic validity, and scientific accuracy of materials appearing in ICA serials.
- To formulate and articulate a direction for the journal/ yearbook during the term of the editorship that is in keeping with the mission established by the ICA Board of Directors and Publications Committee.
- To determine content of the journal through selection and active solicitation of scholarly articles that serve to fulfill that mission.
- To appoint (and mentor) a volunteer editorial staff for editorial continuity.

- To establish an editorial board and procedures for peer review of all manuscripts and to handle the peer review process through all revisions.
- To negotiate institutional support for establishing an onsite editorial office with support staff for handling manuscripts and relevant correspondence.
- To establish special issues, if desired, on specific topics; determine guest editors; issue calls for papers; and oversee the work of guest editors in assembling the issue to ensure that established standards are met.
- To ensure that tone and content of articles meet appropriate academic standards and to uphold the use of APA style (*Publication Manual of the American Psychological Association*, 5th ed.), as adopted for ICA serial publications.
- To communicate with authors on all issues of content, accuracy, and relevance, and resolve any major substance issues with authors.
- To review articles for language that could be legally problematic (i.e., potentially libelous), misleading, or inflammatory.
- To oversee the work of review editors, commentary editors, etc., to ensure that they adhere to these same guidelines.

Once article has been accepted for publication:
- To coordinate with the production office on issues of mutual relevance.
- To obtain and provide the publisher (OUP, Erlbaum) with signed copyright documents from each author when manuscripts for the issue are sent to the production office.
- To adhere to the production schedule established by the production office (in concert with the publisher) in order to meet fiscal and contractual obligations and ensure timely publication and fairness to authors and advertisers.
- To check for errors in factual and statistical information contained in the articles, to query authors about missing information and pursue author queries until resolved, and to verify that all internal references within an article are included in the reference list and vice versa and that all reference information is both complete and correct.
- To make sure that the author has made all agreed-upon changes in the manuscript and provided a disk file that reflects these changes.
- To obtain biographical information on each author and provide a brief biographical sketch to accompany the article.

- To obtain camera-ready hard copies and electronic files of all figures and artwork used in the article.
- To provide the production office and publisher with a table of contents and contact information (including mail and email addresses and phone and fax numbers) for all authors.
- To provide the production office with clean hard copies and disk versions of each article and front matter in MSWord, along with artwork in usable form, on the dates outlined in the production schedule.

Upon receiving page proofs from production office (about 2 months after submission):
- To proofread pages for typographical, formatting, and other errors.
- To check tables and figures for placement and accuracy.

Production Office:
- To coordinate with the production office on issues of mutual relevance.
- To copyedit manuscripts for grammar and typographical accuracy.
- To finetune and ensure adherence to APA style.
- To format articles into that journal's style.
- To send proofs of each article to first authors with correc

tions made and queries noted—offprint order forms are also sent at this time.
- To make authors' corrections and send corrected proofs to the editorial office.
- To make editorial-office corrections and send proofs to publisher for approval.
- To make final corrections, if any, and prepare PDFs in dictated style for printer.
- Prepare PDFs in dictated style for OUP website.

Book/Monograph Authors' and Editors' Responsibilities

The primary author or editor of a book or monograph is responsible for all scholarly and academic aspects of the work. He or she is also responsible for:

1. Ensuring that the work meets the highest standards of scholarly and professional quality.

2. Ensuring the originality of all material in the work for which copyright clearance has not been obtained.

3. Obtaining copyright clearance for any nonoriginal material (quotations, charts, figures, photographs, and other copyrightable work) included that is covered by copyright. If there is a fee for any permission, it must be approved by the ICA Executive Director or commercial publisher

before agreement for use is signed. Copies of all copyright clearances must be filed at ICA headquarters or office of the commercial publisher with the final draft of the manuscript.

4. Running an ICA copyright statement in all material published by ICA: "Copyright ©20XX by the International Communication Association. All rights reserved. No portion of the contents may be reproduced in any form without written permission of the International Communication Association."

5. Assigning copyright for the book or monograph to ICA. The author/editor is responsible for contacting the Executive Director to obtain appropriate copyright assignment forms. Completed forms must be returned to ICA headquarters for filing and distribution to the appropriate copyright office and the commercial publisher.

6. Meeting all deadlines for copy, corrected galleys, and corrected page proofs set by the publisher.

7. Avoiding unnecessary corrections to galleys. Once galleys have been corrected and returned to the publisher, additional corrections on page proofs that have not been made necessary by publisher changes between the galley and page proof stage are chargeable to the author/editor.

8. Including the following sentence in the policy statement or preface to the work: The contents of this publication are the responsibility of its author [or authors] and do not necessarily reflect the official policies or positions of the International Communication Association or its members, officers, or staff.

9. All editors or authors of ICA books and monographs must sign a form acknowledging that they have read the statement of editorial responsibilities and have agreed to abide by the provisions set forth.

Publication Contracts:
Solicitation and Negotiation

The Executive Director will solicit and negotiate bids for publishing ICA serials on behalf of the ICA Board of Directors, who consider and approve publishing contracts.

Renewal Contracts
When the Board of Directors has determined that ICA should enter into a renewal contract with a commercial publisher, university press, or other professional entity, the Executive Director, in consultation with the President and Publications Committee Chair, will negotiate the renewal process, with final approval by the ICA Board of Directors.

New Contracts

When the Board of Directors has determined that ICA should solicit bids from different contractors for publishing one or more of its serials, the Executive Director will draft a formal Request for Proposals (RFP), make it available for review and approval by the Executive Committee, distribute the RFP, and collect all bids. The Executive Director will then distribute copies to the Executive Committee and Publications Committee for review. The Publications Committee will assess each bid in terms of the publisher's ability to satisfy the requiremenets of the Assocation's publications program. With the advice of the Publications Committee, the Executive Committee will (a) evaluate the submissions; (2) select a publisher of choice, and (3) identify those items needing revision, if any, in order to fully satisfy the needs of the Association.

The Executive Director will enter into formal negotiations with the publisher on behalf of the Assocation, keeping the Executive Committee apprised of progress in the negotiation process and seeking its counsel as needed. When the contract has been compleed to the satisfaction of the Executive Committee, the President and Executive Director will sign the contract as the official signatories of the Association.

Adoption or Creation of Serial Publications

Proposing New Journals

Proposals for adoption of an existing journal or creation of a new scholarly publication shall be submitted to the Publications Committee for review, evaluation, and recommendation.

Proposals must include a detailed editorial statement, a rationale for its inclusion in ICA's publication program, and a detailed financial statement and marketing analysis. The Publications Committee will evaluate the proposal on criteria that include but are not limited to the following: consistency with ICA's publication objectives; scholarly needs of the membership; financial viability. The Publications Committee shall forward its recommendation to the ICA Executive Committee for action.

The Executive Committee is empowered to authorize a formal feasibility study. The feasibility study team shall be comprised of the Finance Committee Chair, Publications Committee Chair, and the Executive Director. Should this study conclude that the creation or adoption of a new journal would be in the best interests of the Association, the original proposal, along with the recommendation of the Publications Committee and the results of the feasibility study, shall be submitted to the Board of Directors for action.